CW01467478

MOROCCO TRAVEL GUIDE 2023

Morocco The Perfect Destination for Adventure Seekers, Beach Lovers, and History Buffs

BRENDA SMITH

Copyright © [2023] by [Brenda Smith]

All rights reserved. No part of this publication may be reproduced, distributed, or transmitted in any form or by any means, including photocopying, recording, or other electronic or mechanical methods, without the prior written permission of the publisher, except in the case of brief quotations embodied in critical reviews and certain other noncommercial uses permitted by copyright law.

Learn some Arabic phrases

Resources
Moroccan National Tourist Office website

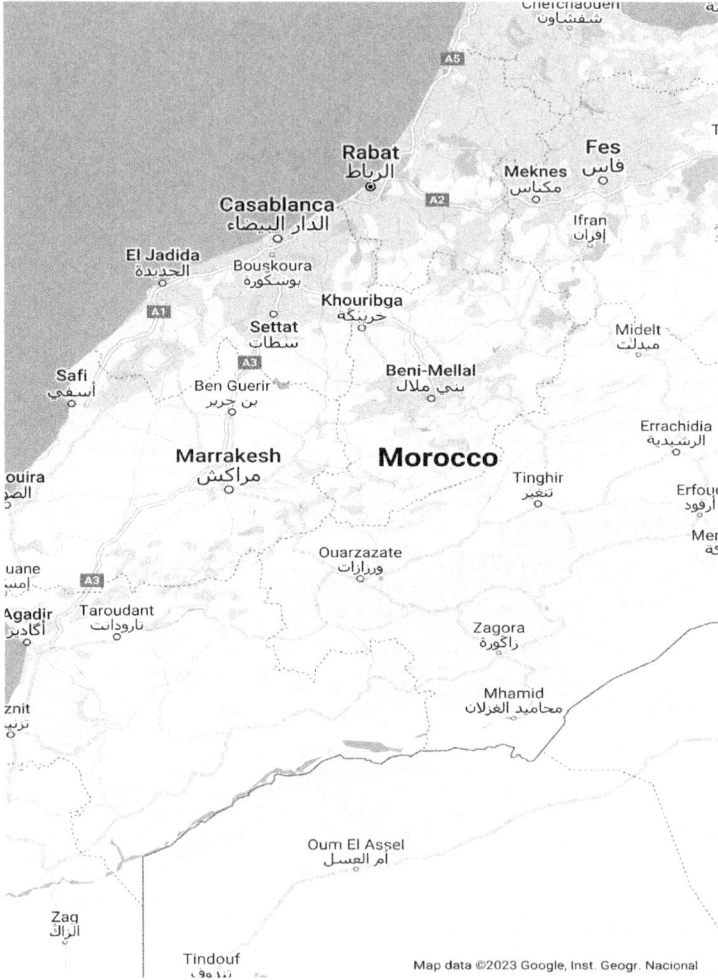

INTRODUCTION

Welcome to the vibrant land of Morocco, where ancient traditions intertwine with modern wonders, creating a tapestry of culture, history, and breathtaking landscapes. Nestled in the northwest corner of Africa, Morocco beckons travelers with its diverse landscapes, from the golden dunes of the Sahara Desert to the snow-capped peaks of the Atlas Mountains and the sun-kissed beaches along the Atlantic coastline.

As you turn the pages of this comprehensive Morocco travel guide, prepare to embark on an unforgettable journey through a country that is as captivating as it is intriguing. Whether you are a seasoned adventurer, a culture enthusiast, a history buff, or simply someone seeking a truly immersive travel experience, Morocco promises to enthrall and enchant you at every turn.

Step foot into the bustling medinas, where the air is alive with the aroma of exotic spices and the vibrant colors of carpets, ceramics, and textiles lure you into a world of craftsmanship. Lose yourself in the labyrinthine streets of ancient cities like Marrakech, Fes, and Chefchaouen, where every corner reveals a new treasure waiting to be discovered.

Immerse yourself in the intoxicating sounds of Moroccan music, the soul-stirring chants of the Gnawa musicians, and the rhythmic beats of the traditional drums. Indulge your taste buds in the tantalizing flavors of Moroccan cuisine, with its aromatic tagines, mouthwatering couscous, and refreshing mint tea.

But Morocco is not just about its captivating cities. Venture into the vast Sahara Desert and witness the spectacle of a Saharan sunset, as the shifting sands create a mesmerizing display of colors that paint the horizon. Experience the nomadic way of life, riding a camel across the dunes and spending a night under the starry desert sky, surrounded by tranquility and the silence of the vast expanse. For the adventure seekers, the Atlas Mountains beckon with their rugged beauty and hidden valleys. Hike to the summit of Mount Toubkal, the highest peak in North Africa, or explore the lush valleys and traditional Berber villages that dot the landscape.

In this guide, we have curated a wealth of information to help you make the most of your Moroccan adventure. From practical tips on transportation and accommodation to insights into the country's rich history and culture, we aim to empower you with the knowledge you need to create your own unforgettable experiences.

So, whether you dream of wandering through the enchanting blue streets of Chefchaouen, bargaining in the bustling souks of Marrakech, or embarking on a trek through the majestic Atlas Mountains, let this Morocco travel guide be your trusted companion, revealing the hidden gems and local secrets that make this country a truly unforgettable destination.

Get ready to immerse yourself in the colors, sounds, and flavors of Morocco - a land where ancient traditions meet modern wonders, and where every moment is infused with the magic of a thousand tales waiting to be told.

CHAPTER 1
Why Visit Morocco in 2023?

Morocco desert

Exploring the Beauty and Magic of the Sahara Desert: A Journey into the Mystical World of Morocco's Desert

A world of infinite horizons awaits you, where time appears to stand still, and the golden sands extend as far as the eye can see. Welcome to Morocco's magnificent Sahara Desert, a breathtaking location that perfectly captures the spirit of exploration, serenity, and amazement.

Morocco's southeast is home to one of the world's most famous and impressive deserts, the Sahara. This desert offers an unmatched experience that will leave you in awe of nature's magnificence with its sweeping dunes, towering sand mountains, and historic camel caravan routes.

Be prepared to experience an ambience beyond description as you begin your desert tour. All who walk into the Sahara's embrace are enchanted by its shifting sands, which produce a constantly moving canvas of undulating forms and patterns.

Your voyage starts with a captivating camel trek into the dunes, where your regal desert companion's rhythmic sway leads you further into this mystical landscape. As you move across the ageless environment, feel the soothing touch of the desert breeze against your skin and pay attention to the sand's quiet humming.

Watch the magic of a Saharan sunset as the sun starts to set, painting the sky with shades of orange, pink, and gold. With its warm embrace of the desert and ethereal brilliance, the horizon creates a scene that is difficult to describe in words. It is a magical event that will leave a lifetime of memories.

Get ready to be astounded by the cosmic music that plays above you as night falls. The Sahara reveals a starry sky, unlike anything you have ever seen because it is far from the light pollution of busy towns. Each glittering dot narrates a tale of ancient civilizations, explorers, and dreamers who once looked to these celestial constellations for direction. As you lay beneath the cosmic canopy of the desert, let yourself be enchanted by the unfathomable grandeur of the cosmos.

Enter a typical desert camp to complete your adventure, and you'll be welcomed into the Berber culture with warmth and generosity. As you eat under a blanket of stars while telling stories and laughing around a roaring bonfire, savour the aromas of real Moroccan food.

The Sahara is notable for its historical and cultural value and natural beauty. The desert is littered with the remains of past civilizations, including intriguing archaeological sites and fortified desert settlements called ksour. Your desert experience will be more fascinating with the addition of these historical relics, which provide a window into Morocco's rich historical tapestry.

The Sahara Desert in Morocco offers an extraordinary experience that will awaken your senses, kindle your spirit of adventure, and leave an everlasting stamp on your soul, whether you decide to go on a multi-day desert tour or a shorter retreat. It is a location where time stands still, allowing you to rediscover the genuine meaning of solitude and peace and to re-establish a connection with the essence of nature.

So embrace the Sahara's charm, where the majesty of the desert is revealed momentarily. Allow yourself to be mesmerized by the remarkable landscape's immensity, silence, and untamed beauty. Your adventure into the heart of the Moroccan desert is waiting, eager to pique your curiosity and disclose its secrets.

The Best Time to Visit Morocco

Timing is everything when organizing a trip to Morocco. The nation's varied landscapes, lively culture, and rich history provide a plethora of adventures all year long. But to fully enjoy your trip, it's crucial to consider the most recent variables affecting the ideal time to visit Morocco.

Morocco has traditionally been visited most frequently in the spring (March to May) and fall (September to November) seasons. The nice weather during these times, which ranges from mild to warm, makes it easy to travel throughout the country's major towns, hike through the Atlas Mountains, and experience the Sahara Desert.

Morocco's weather patterns have changed somewhat due to recent climate changes. The nation is now seeing hotter summers and milder winters, which has altered the conventional wisdom on the ideal time to travel.

It is advised to consider travelling to Morocco in the shoulder seasons of early spring (March to April) and late autumn (October to November) to adjust to these changes. These times of year balance pleasant weather and sparser crowds, enabling a more personal and immersive experience. While missing the busiest tourist season, you can still enjoy the springtime landscapes in bloom or the spectacular autumnal colours.

It's also important to note that Morocco is a sizable nation with a varied landscape. The best time to go depends on each region's microclimate and distinctive attractions. For instance:

Coastal Regions: The climate is generally milder towards the shore, especially in cities like Casablanca, Rabat, and Essaouira. Sea breezes might help during the hot summer months. As a result, virtually the entire year can be spent visiting these areas.

Atlas Mountains: Late spring or early fall are the finest times to visit the Atlas Mountains and trek Mount Toubkal, the highest peak in

North Africa. At these times, the weather is suitable for outdoor activities.

Sahara Desert: During the summer, the Sahara Desert can reach temperatures above 40°C (104°F). It is advised to travel during the cooler seasons, such as late fall or early spring, to avoid the intense heat. You may experience camel treks, nighttime camping in the desert, and stargazing without discomfort. It's crucial to remember that Morocco is a riveting location all year round, despite the shifting weather patterns. There are ways to make the most of your trip, even in the sweltering summer months, such as visiting the cooler coastline districts or higher altitude destinations like the highlands.

As a result of climate change, the ideal season to visit Morocco has changed. Even while the typical spring and fall seasons still offer great weather, taking into account the shoulder seasons might give a more personalized experience with fewer tourists. Your optimum travel period will ultimately rely on the places you intend to explore and your personal preferences for the weather and visitor activity. Morocco will impress you with its captivating fusion of history, culture, and natural beauty regardless of the season if you prepare appropriately.

What to Pack for Your Morocco Trip

Packaging wisely for your amazing vacation to Morocco is essential to guarantee a relaxing and delightful stay. Morocco's varied landscapes, energetic towns, and rich culture necessitate a carefully considered packing list. Here's a convincing update on what to bring with you to Morocco:

Clothing:

Pack lightweight, breathable clothing for Morocco because the country enjoys a wide range of temperatures. Cotton and linen are good choices for hot days.

Dress modestly: Respecting the community is crucial, especially in rural and religious settings. Dress modestly by bringing loose-fitting, knee- and shoulder-covering apparel.

Bring a sweater or lightweight jacket to layer up in the chilly evenings and mountainous areas.

Cosy shoes:

Shoes for walking: The streets and medinas of Morocco frequently have uneven surfaces and cobblestones. For sightseeing, choose a pair of comfortable walking shoes or sneakers.

Sandals: Open-toed sandals are ideal for warm weather and are simple to take off when visiting mosques or private residences.

Travel necessities:

Passport validity: Verify that your passport has at least six months left.

Check your country's requirements for a visa before travelling.

Morocco employs two-pin plugs that are similar to those used in Europe. Therefore, a universal travel adapter will be useful.

Carry a variety of cards and cash in your wallet. Although there are many ATMs in towns, having some Moroccan dirhams on hand is a good idea, particularly in rural areas.

Items for Personal Care:

Wear a hat and sunscreen to protect yourself from the harsh Moroccan sun, especially in the desert.

If you use any prescription medication, ensure you have a sufficient quantity on hand and the required prescriptions.

Toiletries: Bring the essentials, such as your toothbrush, toothpaste, shampoo, and any other personal care products you might need. If you'd rather purchase these things locally, they are easily accessible in cities.

Accessories for travel:

A daypack or tiny backpack is practical for day travel because it can hold your camera, water, and snacks.

A lightweight, quick-drying travel towel is useful for trips to the beach and shared lodgings.

Use locks on your daypack and luggage to protect your possessions when travelling.

Keep your gadgets charged and connected throughout your journey by carrying a portable charger.

Miscellaneous:

Basic medical items, including bandages, antiseptic cream, painkillers, and any prescribed drugs, should be included in a first aid bag.

Use insect repellent: Mosquitoes and other insects, particularly in rural regions, may be present depending on the area and the time of year.

Travel guidebook: To better comprehend Morocco's history, culture, and tourist attractions, think about packing a guidebook or downloading a travel app.

To adjust your packing list, remember to check the weather prediction for the Morocco trip dates and locations you will visit. Additionally, it's a good idea to pack lightly and leave room in your luggage for any souvenirs and other finds you make along the journey. Travel safely.

Getting Around Morocco

Travelling in Morocco is a fascinating journey through a complex tapestry of cultural experiences and various landscapes. Exploring this magnificent country is easy and rewarding because of the sophisticated transportation infrastructure and the range of options available.

In Morocco, trains are one of the most popular ways of transportation. An effective means to move between the country's major cities is by rail, which connects Casablanca, Marrakech, Fes, and Rabat, among others. Most of the time, trains are dependable and comfortable and offer first-class and economical options to accommodate different price ranges.

Bus travel is another well-liked method of moving about Morocco. A bus network is a fantastic option for travelling to smaller towns and villages because it serves both urban and rural areas. With frequent departures and various routes, numerous bus companies run nationwide. Buses offer a chance to meet locals and other passengers and are typically inexpensive.

Hiring a car or a motorcycle is a great option for individuals looking for a more daring adventure. Morocco has a comprehensive road system linking its major towns and tourist destinations. Renting a car gives you flexibility and the ability to go at your leisure while discovering off-the-beaten-path locations. Driving in Morocco can be difficult, especially in crowded cities. Therefore, it's crucial to remember to be cautious and protective.

Taxis are a practical mode of transportation in cities. Metered and shared taxis are available in larger cities like Casablanca and Marrakech. While shared taxis follow set routes and pick up passengers along the way, they are more economical than metered taxis and use a fare calculator to ensure clear pricing. It's customary to haggle over prices, so settling on a price before the trip begins is crucial.

Walking is frequently the greatest way to explore the colourful ambience and find hidden jewels when exploring the picturesque medinas or old neighbourhoods. Cities in

Morocco are renowned for their winding streets lined with vibrant markets, lively souks, and magnificent architecture. By exploring on foot, you should appreciate each area's subtle intricacies and distinctive characteristics.

Lastly, Morocco is well known for its magnificent scenery, including the Atlas Mountains, the Sahara Desert, and the stunning coastline areas. It is advised to take domestic flights or scheduled tours to reach these natural beauties. Domestic flights connect major cities and greatly shorten travel times. Guided tours, on the other hand, offer a hassle-free opportunity to discover Morocco's varied geography and frequently include lodging, transportation, and knowledgeable guides.

CHAPTER 2

Top Destinations in Morocco

Essaouira Morocco

Essaouira, Morocco, a captivating coastal city, continues to enchant visitors with its unique blend of history, culture, and natural beauty. Nestled on the Atlantic coastline, Essaouira is a haven that seamlessly combines old-world charm with a vibrant contemporary atmosphere.

Renowned for its well-preserved medina, Essaouira transports you back as you wander through its narrow streets and bustling souks. The medina's distinctive blue and white buildings, adorned with ornate wooden doors and window frames, create a picturesque, charming, and mesmerizing backdrop.

This UNESCO World Heritage site is a living testament to the city's rich history, having witnessed the influence of various civilizations throughout the centuries.

One of the city's most iconic features is its impressive ramparts, which encircle the medina and offer breathtaking panoramic views of the Atlantic Ocean. Visitors can marvel at the crashing waves atop the fortified walls, watch local fishermen navigating their blue boats, and soak in the refreshing sea breeze.

Beyond its historic allure, Essaouira is also a vibrant hub of artistic expression. The city has long been a magnet for creative souls, attracting musicians, painters, and artisans worldwide. The annual Gnaoua World Music Festival in Essaouira celebrates traditional Moroccan music, featuring captivating performances against the city's charming streets. The medina's numerous art galleries and workshops are a testament to the city's thriving artistic community, offering visitors a chance to explore and appreciate local craftsmanship.

For those seeking outdoor adventures, Essaouira's stunning beaches provide a haven for water sports enthusiasts. The city is renowned for its consistent winds, making it a popular breeze and kite surfing destination. Whether you're an experienced surfer or a beginner looking to try something new, Essaouira's sandy shores and inviting waters offer an ideal playground for aquatic adventures.

Essaouira's culinary scene is a delightful fusion of flavours that reflects the city's diverse cultural heritage. From savouring freshly caught seafood at the bustling port to exploring the aromatic spices and traditional Moroccan dishes in local restaurants, visitors can embark on a gastronomic journey that tantalizes their taste buds and showcases the region's culinary prowess.

The Sahara Desert

Travellers worldwide are drawn to the Sahara Desert, especially in the beautiful country of Morocco. The Moroccan Sahara, located in North Africa, is a fascinating example of how a rich cultural past coexists with natural beauty. This area of the Sahara embodies the stereotype of huge desert terrain, yet it also exhibits distinctive qualities that make it stand out.

The Sahara region of Morocco contains a variety of landscapes, including dunes that tower over the horizon, rocky plateaus, and shifting sands.

Visitors are enthralled by the most famous dunes, such as those at Merzouga and Erg Chebbi, because of their imposing heights and the mesmerizing dance of light and shadow at sunrise and dusk. These mighty dunes provide a spectacular backdrop for those looking for an idyllic getaway from the bustle of daily life, photographers, and adventurers.

Beyond its breathtaking scenery, the Moroccan Sahara is home to diverse cultural traditions. Numerous indigenous nomadic groups call it home, including the Berber people, who have long flourished in this harsh climate. Their habits, customs, and distinctive way of life reflect a strong affinity for the desert. Visitors to the Moroccan Sahara can interact with these communities and learn about their businesses, history, and welcoming nature.

Exploring the Moroccan Sahara includes more than just dunes; buried gems are just waiting to be found. Natural wonders like oasis-like valleys and palm groves emerge amid the environment's appearance of inhospitality, fed by underground rivers and ancient water sources. For instance, the Draa Valley displays a beautiful green corridor slicing across the dry environment, where date palms and productive farms flourish. These oases of lush life offer a beautiful contrast to the desert surrounding them and provide a haven for both people and wildlife.

The Sahara in Morocco also provides access to adventure and discovery. The Bedouin way of navigating the dunes on exhilarating camel excursions allows tourists to experience the rhythms of the desert. They can also partake in exciting sports like sandboarding, gliding down the dunes' smooth slopes, or 4x4 off-road excursions, where they can travel far into the heart of the desert and see its unadulterated beauty firsthand.

Morocco has achieved tremendous advancements in Sahara sustainable tourism standards in recent years. There are now initiatives aimed towards responsible desert travel that strongly emphasize local community empowerment, the preservation of sensitive ecosystems, and cultural appreciation. Visitors may aid in preserving this special ecosystem and its cultural history for future generations by participating in eco-friendly activities and buying locally.

The Atlas Mountains

The Atlas Mountains in North Africa have long fascinated travellers and adventurers due to their untamed beauty and extensive cultural history. These magnificent mountains, which straddle Morocco, Algeria, and Tunisia, have a fascinating tale.

The Atlas Mountains result from millions of years of geological action, rising like a natural fortress. The High Atlas, Middle Atlas, and Anti-Atlas are only a few of the many ranges that make them up. Each has its special traits. One of the tallest mountains in Africa, the High Atlas peaks rise above 4,000 meters (13,000 feet) in altitude.

The region's ecology and climate benefit greatly from the influence of the Atlas Mountains. As a result of their high summits blocking moisture-laden breezes from the

Atlantic Ocean, rain is produced. As a result, while the southern slopes of the Alps are more arid and desert-like, the northern slopes are comparatively lush and home to a variety of flora and wildlife.

Beyond their natural significance, the Atlas Mountains play a significant role in the Berber culture that has existed in the area for millennia. The Berber populations have a deep connection to the soil and have evolved sustainable farming methods to cope with the steep terrain. Their inventiveness and tenacity are demonstrated by their distinctive style of life, which includes terraced fields cut into the slopes and mud-brick settlements clinging to the sides.

The Atlas Mountains still draw tourists from all over the world today. Adventurers travel here to test their limits on exhilarating treks and climbs while immersing themselves in the breathtaking scenery. The mountains provide chances for various outdoor pursuits, including hiking, skiing, mountain biking, and even paragliding, which can lead to life-changing events.

Exploring the Atlas Mountains' rich cultural legacy is another benefit. Visitors are warmly welcomed by the Berber villages, who share details about their customs, music, and cuisine. In traditional towns like Imlil, visitors may experience the wonderful Berber hospitality while learning about the residents' way of life and traditions. Mountain guesthouses called "kasbahs" are also available for travellers.

Additionally, the Atlas Mountains are home to numerous historic archaeological sites, including the well-known Roman remains of

Volubilis in Morocco. These artefacts from earlier civilizations serve as a reminder of the area's historical significance as a hub for trade and cultural exchange.

The ecological importance of the Atlas Mountains and the necessity of conservation initiatives have recently come to light. Endangered species like the Barbary macaque and the Atlas cedar, which are both protected and act as gauges of the ecological health of the mountains, are found in their various ecosystems.

CHAPTER 3

Things to Do in Morocco

Explore the medinas (old cities)

A fascinating journey through time and an immersion in the rich fabric of history, culture, and customs may be had by exploring the medinas or old cities. These historic urban labyrinths still enthral travellers because of their everlasting appeal and magical atmosphere.

Entering a medina is like entering a living museum, where the twisting, winding alleyways and labyrinthine alleys conceal the mysteries of an earlier time. Each medina has its personality and a rich history that captures the cultures and civilizations that have shaped it over centuries.

As you explore the medina's souks or bustling markets, your senses are heightened by an explosion of colours, scents, and noises. Exotic spices, fragrant oils, mouthwatering regional specialities, and complex handicrafts and textiles are all exhibited in the bustling kiosks. Working carefully on their works are the talented artisans who have perfected their trades for decades, giving the atmosphere of authenticity and quality.

As you go farther into the medina, you'll come across magnificent architectural marvels, including enormous mosques, opulent palaces, and secret courtyards with exquisite carvings and intricate tilework. The structures themselves are evidence of the expert craftsmanship and distinctive fusion of architectural styles that have developed through the years, blending elements from diverse civilizations, including Arab, Moorish, and Ottoman.

Connecting with the residents and seeing their way of life is one of the medinas' most alluring features. You will see pleasant people, hear children playing and laughing, and see daily customs and rituals passed down through the years as you navigate the little streets. By interacting with them, you can better comprehend the people's customs, traditions, and cultural significance of the medina.

The medinas are rooted in heritage but embrace modernity, fusing the two seamlessly. Modern galleries, chic shops, and inviting cafes are among the historic buildings. You may enjoy the enduring beauty while sipping traditional mint tea in one of these establishments.

Exploring the medinas is more than just a sightseeing excursion; it's a deeply moving cultural encounter that transports you to another time and space. This is an opportunity to recognize the communities who have protected these historical treasures and their resiliency in the face of constant external change

Visit ancient ruins

Exploring ancient ruins is a fascinating and educational experience that enables us to learn about lost civilizations' secrets. Our ancestors' inventiveness, creativity, and cultural accomplishments are displayed in these ancient places, which provide a window into the rich fabric of human history. We set out on a transforming adventure as we investigate these mysterious relics of the past, one that not only expands our knowledge of previous civilizations but also builds a strong bond with our shared history. In this revised explanation, We explore why exploring ancient ruins is still a fascinating and worthwhile activity in the present era.

Preservation of Cultural Legacy: Our cultural legacy can be physically accessed through ancient ruins. They provide a chance to travel back in time and experience directly the wonders of human ingenuity. Whether they are ancient cities, temples, or archaeological sites, these locations are of immeasurable historical and cultural value. We actively support their preservation and the maintenance of our shared legacy for future generations by visiting and admiring these remains.

Unravel the Mysteries: The mystery surrounding ancient ruins is one of its most alluring features. The original purpose, building methods, and societal context of many of these sites—many of which have weathered the passage of time—remain frequently unknown. Archaeologists and historians eventually solve the puzzles surrounding these perplexing remnants as we investigate and analyze them, connecting together pieces of the past. Visitors can participate in this fascinating process, working with professionals to find and decipher hints and add to our understanding of these ancient civilizations.

Visits to ancient ruins generate a strong sense of connection with the civilizations that once called these magnificent locations home. A strong empathic connection is evoked by following in their footsteps, admiring their architectural accomplishments, and observing the remains of their daily lives. This comprehensive encounter gives us a great understanding of their challenges, victories, and legacy. It serves as a reminder that, despite the passage of time, we are all connected by a single thread of humanity and that our histories are intertwined with that of others.

Ancient ruins have long been a source of creativity and imagination for writers, artists, and other creatives. These magnificent buildings spark our imaginations and carry us to far-off places and times. Their majesty, elaborate designs, and aesthetic motifs have affected numerous historical pieces of literature, art, and architecture. We tap into this source of creativity by touring historic sites; this sparks our imagination and broadens our horizons.

The breadth of human achievement and the fleeting nature of life are two things that visiting ancient ruins makes us think about. These locations document empires' expansion and decline, civilizations' tenacity, and the ebb and flow of human development. They prompt us to think about the lessons we might take from those who came before us and serve as a reminder of the transience of our societies. We are humbled, inspired, and motivated to add to the ongoing story of humanity in the face of their enormous accomplishments.

Camel trekking in the Sahara Desert

Camel trekking in the Moroccan Sahara Desert is a remarkable experience that transports you through one of the most beautiful environments in the world. It provides a special chance to fully immerse in the area's rich history, vibrant culture, and breathtaking natural beauty.

You'll be taken back in time as you start your camel trek by following in the footsteps of the early explorers and traders who crossed these dunes hundreds of years ago. The Sahara Desert presents a stunning backdrop that appears unaffected by the passage of time with its wide expanse of golden sand and towering dunes.

The adventure starts when you first meet your friendly and dependable camel companions, called the "ships of the desert." These gorgeous animals make the ideal travel companions because of their prowess in navigating treacherous terrain and their long history of living in the desert. As you learn how to mount, dismount, and converse with your camel, you'll rapidly form a special bond with it. This bond will give your journey an additional element of magic.

You'll learn about the actual essence of desert life as you travel into the wide desert under the guidance of knowledgeable local Bedouin guides. You can escape the stress of modern life by taking in the rhythmic sway of the camels' movement and the stillness of the desert. You may unplug from the outside world and reconnect with nature in the desert because of its peace and tranquillity.

New experiences and stunning sights await you every day. As far as the eye can reach, spectacular dunes will be crossed, their shapes continually changing due to the wind. You are left in amazement by the striking contrasts of the desert landscape, which range from the warm ochre tones of the sand to the deep blue of the sky.

Along the route, you'll come across an isolated oasis where luscious palm groves appear out of nowhere in the desert, like mirages. In addition to affording shade and a chance to rest and recharge before resuming your journey, these green havens give you a much-needed break.

The desert transforms stunningly as the sun sets over the horizon, painting the sky with a vibrant palette of oranges, pinks, and purples. Stars start to sparkle in the great expanse overhead as the once-scalding heat gradually gives way to a pleasant cold. The brilliance of the celestial sky will enthral you in the stillness of the night, surrounded by the silence of the desert, distant from the light pollution of cities.

You'll have the chance to speak with the local Berber populations during your camel trip, who have a long-standing affinity for the desert. You'll obtain a deep understanding of their way of life and the rich cultural history that thrives in this challenging yet beautiful environment by sharing stories, customs, and meals around a campfire.

Camel trekking in the Moroccan Sahara Desert is a memorable experience that awakens the senses and the soul. It provides an opportunity to unplug from the outside world, get back in touch with nature, and enjoy life's simple joys. Whether you set out on a brief trip or a lengthy one, the appeal of the desert and the magic of the camel will leave a lasting impression on your heart and serve as a constant reminder of the beauty that can be found when we embrace the uncharted and travel into the wild.

Swim in the Atlantic Ocean

An unforgettable and energizing experience, swimming in the Atlantic Ocean is unlike any other. You join a spectacular environment teeming with untamed beauty as you submerge yourself in the expanse of this magnificent body of water.

Visualize yourself diving into the beautiful, crystal-clear waters off the Atlantic coast. You can immediately feel the chill as soon as your toes enter the water, which is in sharp contrast to the warmth of the sun's rays as they kiss your skin. The ocean welcomes you as you go on your adventure and invites you to discover its secret depths.

As you travel farther into the Atlantic, a staggering variety of marine life will be found. Schools of colourful tropical fish swirl under you, their palettes rivalling any artist.

Graceful dolphins will join you as you glide over the water, their playful curiosity serving as a reminder of the wonder and brilliance of these extraordinary animals.

Looking closely, you could see a majestic sea turtle, a representation of endurance and knowledge, delicately navigating the currents. And if you're very lucky, you might even see the majestic humpback whales breaching the surface with their breathtaking displays of strength and grace.

However, it's not simply the marine life that captures your attention; it's also the Atlantic Ocean's sheer size. The sobering grandeur that stretches out in all directions strikes you as you swim. The seemingly endless horizon is a constant reminder of the limitless opportunities and the unrealized potential that resides inside you.

The history and culture of the Atlantic Ocean are very rich. These waters have inspired countless tales of discovery and adventure. You are following in the footsteps of those who dared to dream large and tackle the uncharted, from Christopher Columbus' fabled expeditions to the New World to the intrepid explorers who crossed the ocean in quest of new frontiers.

You might discover yourself surrounded by the remains of history itself if you keep swimming. Shipwrecks, submerged deep beneath the waters, reveal the history of trade routes, naval conquests, and the tenacity of the human spirit. A monument to the unquenchable human thirst for exploration and discovery, each sunken vessel contains mysteries just waiting to be found.

Aside from being an adventure, swimming in the Atlantic Ocean offers a chance to connect with history, nature, and your sense of awe. It's an opportunity to appreciate the ocean's strength and size while being reminded of your place in it and the countless options available.

Please take a deep breath, jump in, and let the Atlantic Ocean reveal its mysteries to you the next time you find yourself standing on the Atlantic coastline. You'll emerge from its depths transformed, carrying with you the memories of a once-in-a-lifetime experience that will uplift and inspire you for the rest of your days.

Learn about Moroccan culture

Moroccan culture is a lively tapestry made of the country's long history, numerous customs, and an intriguing fusion of influences from various civilizations. A fascinating mosaic of traditions, art forms, food, and social behaviours has been created in Morocco due to the unique combination of Arab, Berber, African, and European elements. This immersion in Moroccan culture is similar to taking an enthralling voyage.

Moroccan culture is known for its warmth and hospitality, one of its most characteristic features. Travellers will find Morocco a very welcome place because Moroccans are renowned for their genuine warmth and enthusiasm in greeting guests. Moroccan culture places a high value on hospitality, and visitors are frequently treated like family while enjoying hearty quantities of mint tea and mouthwatering regional cuisines like couscous or tagine.

Morocco's unique cultural legacy has been influenced by its location and history. The country is home to various scenery, including the majestic Atlas Mountains, the charming

Sahara Desert, and the breathtaking coastline regions. Morocco is a culturally diverse country with distinctive traditions, dialects, and art forms in each area.

Moroccan culture places a specific emphasis on art and craftsmanship. The nation is known for its elaborate architecture, colourful mosaics, and excellent handicrafts. As UNESCO World Heritage Sites, the medinas (ancient city quarters) of cities like Marrakech, Fez, and Chefchaouen provide a captivating view of the nation's architectural grandeur. Moroccan artisans are extremely accomplished in various crafts, including metalwork, leatherwork, carpet weaving, and pottery, and they produce exquisite designs that represent the nation's cultural character.

Its cuisine is another unique facet of Moroccan culture that appeals to the senses. It is a wonderful fusion of flavours and spices that draws on Mediterranean, Arab, and Berber culinary traditions. The classic tagine, a slow-cooked stew of meat or vegetables with flavorful sauces, best represents Moroccan cuisine. Couscous, pastilla (a savoury pastry stuffed with beef and almonds), and a variety of mouthwatering sweets like baklava and chakra are all popular dishes.

Moroccan music and dance styles also display the country's diverse culture. The heartfelt melodies of the oud, a stringed instrument, the rhythmic beats of the darbuka, a type of drum, and the alluring vocals of Moroccan singers define traditional music. The vibrant "Ahidous" folk dance is performed at festivities and weddings, and belly dancers' mesmerizing motions give an enticing element to the cultural fabric.

Islam is the most prevalent religion, and religion and spirituality are strongly rooted in Moroccan society. Mosques serve as places of worship and architectural wonders, such as the stunning Hassan II Mosque in Casablanca. From the call to prayer resonating through the streets to celebrating religious festivals like Ramadan and Eid, Islamic traditions and rituals are ingrained in daily life.

In summary, studying Moroccan culture is a fascinating investigation that reveals the facets of a multicultural, welcoming, and culturally active country. Morocco offers a captivating experience that embraces the beauty of cultural fusion and invites you to submerge yourself in a world of enchantment, from the warm smiles of its people to the beautiful designs decorating its architecture, the savoury foods, and the soul-stirring music.

Sample the local cuisine

Trying the local cuisine is necessary to get a true sense of Morocco. Morocco is known for its extensive and varied culinary traditions. These traditions were influenced by the Berber, Arab, and Mediterranean cultures, creating a distinct and savoury cuisine.

The enormous variety of aromatic spices employed in Moroccan cuisine is a key draw for eating there. Moroccan food tantalizes the taste buds and creates a symphony of flavours, from the warm and earthy tones of cumin and turmeric to the zesty bite of paprika and ginger. Moroccan cuisine is a wonderful joy for the tongue and the body because these spices provide the meal's depth and complexity and a host of health advantages.

Moroccan food is also a celebration of locally grown and fresh ingredients. The nation's proximity to the Mediterranean Sea guarantees a plentiful supply of seafood delicacies, and its rich fields yield an astounding range of fruits, vegetables, and aromatic herbs. Each ingredient, whether it is the delectable olives, the juicy tomatoes, the fragrant mint, or the renowned argan oil, is carefully chosen and mixed to produce a dish with flavours and textures that are harmonious and accurately reflect the lively culture and geography of Morocco.

The tagine, a traditional clay pot in which various meats, vegetables, and spices are slow-cooked to perfection, is a noteworthy highlight of Moroccan cuisine. This cooking technique enables the flavours to combine, producing soft, melt-in-your-mouth dishes full of distinctive Moroccan flavours. Several variants suit various dietary needs, ranging from the traditional lamb tagine with prunes and almonds to the vegetarian-friendly chickpea and veggie tagine.

Additionally well-known is the street cuisine culture in Morocco. You'll come across various delectable snacks and delicacies as you stroll through the busy marketplaces and lively streets. Try the flavorful Bastille, a thin pastry stuffed with layers of spiced meat or veggies and sprinkled with powdered sugar and cinnamon for a delicious fusion of sweet and savoury tastes. Enjoy the delightful kebabs expertly grilled with the freshly baked khobz (bread). Don't forget to try some traditional Moroccan mint tea, a flavorful beverage regarded as a sign of friendliness and hospitality.

In addition to the delicious food, eating together is a very important cultural practice in Morocco. The idea of "source," a communal dining experience where family and friends gather around a table and share not only food but also tales, laughter, and a sense of togetherness, is something the Moroccan people take pride in. By consuming the regional food, you become fully immersed in Moroccan culture and develop deep bonds with the people that live in this alluring nation.

Shop for souvenirs

Morocco is a veritable gold mine when it comes to souvenir buying. The nation provides travellers looking for souvenirs with a distinctive and captivating experience thanks to its rich cultural past, lively markets, and talented artists. Here are some persuasive arguments in favour of souvenir shopping in **Morocco:**

Authenticity: Moroccan artistry is renowned for upholding the ancient methods handed down through the years. You aren't just buying a mass-produced object when you buy souvenirs in Morocco; you are also obtaining a piece of Moroccan culture and history. Each piece is painstakingly created, displaying the nation's artistic heritage and meticulousness.

Morocco offers a wide variety of souvenirs that appeal to a variety of tastes and interests. There is plenty to satisfy everyone's tastes, including fine jewellery, delicate craftsmanship, traditional leather products, and rugs and carpets with elaborate designs. Morocco has everything, whether you're interested in accessories, home design, or fashion.

Experience the Souks: The vibrant markets, or souks, are essential to Moroccan culture and a must-see for any traveller. The exploration of these bustling markets is an adventure in and of itself. Stroll through confined passageways, you will encounter various sights, sounds, and smells. A unique shopping experience you won't find anywhere else is created by the vibrant atmosphere, negotiating with vendors, and finding hidden gems.

Supporting Local Craftsmen: When you buy souvenirs in Morocco, you directly support the livelihoods of the country's craftsmen and artisans. These gifted people rely on their abilities and imagination to support their families and uphold artisan traditions. Your purchases positively affect the towns you visit by preserving these antiquated practices and boosting the local economy.

Cultural Insight: Moroccan souvenir shopping provides an opportunity to learn more about the nation's rich cultural legacy. Many artists are delighted to tell their tales and explain the meaning behind their works of art. You may learn more about the historical significance of traditional jewellery designs, the meaning woven into Berber rugs, the beautiful geometric patterns gracing Moroccan tiles, etc. It's an opportunity to interact with locals, discover their customs, and appreciate the nation's artistic legacy.

Gifts to Remember: Moroccan trinkets offer thoughtful presents that your loved ones will treasure. Whether it's a handwoven rug, original pottery, or a stunning leather purse, these gifts will take your loved ones back to Morocco with a sense of authenticity and exoticism. These presents will be valued for their originality and sensitivity, leaving a lasting impression on your trips.

As a result of its authenticity, a wide variety of souvenirs, immersive souk culture, support for regional artisans, cultural insights, and the chance to provide thoughtful gifts, souvenir shopping in Morocco is a fascinating experience. It's an opportunity to incorporate Morocco's vivid culture and artistry into your

life, assist neighbourhood organizations, and
uphold   long-standing   customs.

CHAPTER 4

Travel Tips

Stay safe in Morocco

Prioritizing your safety is essential for a memorable and pleasurable experience in Morocco. Here are some safety recommendations for your trip to this stunning North African nation:

Plan by doing extensive research on the Moroccan regions you intend to visit before your trip. To prevent inadvertent violations, familiarize oneself with the local laws, customs, and traditions. Learn about the possible dangers and security issues in particular areas to make wise selections.

Dress Properly: Morocco has strict cultural norms and a large Muslim population. Dress modestly, especially while visiting rural areas and religious locations, to show respect and fit in with the locals. Avoid wearing anything too revealing, and think about always having a scarf or shawl with you to cover your head or shoulders.

Transportation Security: Be watchful of your possessions and hide expensive goods when taking public transportation, such as buses or trains. Ensure the car is in good condition and obey all traffic laws if you rent one. It is also advised to select trusted taxi services or pre-arranged transportation choices to reduce the danger of fraud.

Although Morocco is typically a safe country, it is advisable to use caution when handling your money and possessions. Keep your cash, passport, and other critical documents concealed and close to your body by wearing a money belt or other safe bag. To prevent unwanted attention, consider leaving valuable jewellery and superfluous electronics at home.

Bargaining and Street Sellers: Morocco is renowned for its vibrant markets and street sellers. Be watchful of pickpockets while participating in this bustling retail culture, and always keep an eye on your stuff. Be kind but forceful while haggling, and always discuss prices before making a transaction.

Food and Water Safety: Stick to bottled water and avoid tap water, ice cubes, and raw foods that may have been washed with tap water to prevent health problems while travelling. To reduce the danger of foodborne infections, choose meals that have been properly cooked and dine at recognized restaurants and cafés.

To stay in touch in an emergency, ensure you can access communication tools like a local SIM card or an international roaming plan. Save crucial phone numbers, such as those for the neighbourhood embassy or consulate, emergency services, and your lodging.

Solo travellers should take extra precautions and stay off the streets late at night in unfamiliar locations if they travel alone. Stay in well-known and popular sites, and for added safety and local knowledge, think about going on group excursions or hiring a reliable local guide.

Cultural Sensitivity: When photographing people, especially in more conservative locations, respect the community's traditions by getting their consent first. Be aware of cultural differences and refrain from discussing or participating in sensitive or divisive political issues.

Above all, trust your gut instincts, and keep yourself aware of your surroundings. Get out of a situation if it makes you feel unsafe or uneasy. Most Moroccans are kind and friendly, but as in any place, it's important to exercise caution and put your safety first.

Remember that these travel suggestions are intended to improve your security and overall Moroccan experience. You can make enduring memories while discovering this magical country's amazing sights, sounds, and flavours by exercising proper caution and remembrance of the local culture.

Be aware of your surroundings

Being conscious of your surroundings is essential for a safe and happy trip to Morocco. This alluring nation in North Africa is renowned for its bustling cities, varied landscapes, and rich cultural heritage. It's crucial to remain alert and aware of your surroundings to take full advantage of what Morocco offers. Here is a strong justification for the significance of awareness:

Cultural Sensitivity: Morocco is a nation steeped in Islamic principles and customs. Being aware of your surroundings allows you to respect and value the local way of life. Pay attention to the clothing code in the area, especially in more traditional locations, and consider how you act and engage with the populace. This knowledge will prevent unintentionally offending someone and create positive relationships.

Medina Labyrinth Navigation: The medinas, or old town sections, in towns like Marrakech and Fes are beautiful labyrinths of winding lanes and active markets. In these colourful yet complicated settings, becoming lost or disoriented is simple. By remaining vigilant, you may move through the medinas with more assurance, finding your way and averting potential frauds or pickpocketing events. Watch for landmarks, use trustworthy maps, and use caution while taking help from strangers.

Road Safety: Driving in Morocco can be difficult, particularly in crowded city centres or along twisting mountain roads. For your safety, while driving or walking, you must pay attention to your surroundings. Pay attention to pedestrian crossings, irregular driving, and traffic regulations. Additionally, Morocco is well recognized for its variety of modes of transportation, including donkey carts and horse-drawn carriages, both of which call for particular vigilance.

Personal Security: Like any other tourist destination, keeping yourself safe in Morocco requires being aware of your surroundings. Even while travelling to Morocco is typically safe, it's still important to exercise caution. Pay attention, conceal expensive stuff, and take safe transportation in busy places. By exercising caution, you may reduce the likelihood of minor crimes and guarantee a worry-free trip.

Moroccan landscapes, including the Sahara Desert, the Atlas Mountains, and coastal areas, are stunning. Awareness of your surroundings is essential for your safety, whether trekking in the mountains or visiting far-flung desert regions. Learn about the topography, the weather, and potential dangers like wildlife encounters or unexpected environmental changes. Thanks to this awareness, you can ethically and safely take in the splendour of Morocco's natural beauties.

You can experience Morocco's unique culture, navigate its maze-like towns, stay safe on the roads, safeguard your security, and take in its breathtaking natural beauty by being aware of your surroundings. With these perceptions and mindfulness, you may ensure a memorable and secure trip while completely immersing yourself in the attractiveness of this alluring location.

Bargain for souvenirs

Morocco, a country of vivid hues, illustrious traditions, and excellent craftsmanship, offers a beguiling variety of gifts that delight tourists worldwide. The Moroccan market, or souk, entices tourists with its riches, which range from delicate handmade rugs and pottery to traditional leather goods and flavorful spices. Engaging in the art of haggling becomes a necessary component of the voyage to appreciate this ancient land's magic fully.

In Morocco, haggling is more than just about obtaining the greatest deal; it's also about connecting with the locals, learning about their culture, and appreciating the quality and craftsmanship of each object. The following is a convincing justification for why haggling for souvenirs in Morocco is an essential component of the journey:

Keeping Age-Old Traditions Alive: Moroccan markets are a living example of the nation's long-standing artisanal traditions. Each item in the souk is created by talented craftspeople who learned their trade from their ancestors. You play a direct role in the maintenance of these customs via bargaining. Your readiness to partake in this customary ritual demonstrates respect for the skill required and the worth of their cultural legacy.

Cultural Connection and Exchange: Bargaining in Morocco is not just about bargaining over costs; it also serves as a forum for cross-cultural interactions. You can learn about Moroccan customs, hear enthralling tales, and gain insights into the local way of life while negotiating amicably with neighbourhood merchants. By connecting you and the merchants, the procedure helps to bridge the gap between the two worlds and promotes respect and understanding of various cultures.

Adopting the Moroccan Way of Life: Bargaining is integral to Moroccan culture. It's a social exchange that happens throughout routine business dealings. By engaging in this activity, you become fully immersed in the community, accepting their way of life and getting to know Morocco deeper. Instead of being a spectator, you actively participate, and the souk changes into a lively stage where memories are created.

Finding Unique and Authentic Treasures: The Moroccan souk has many unique and genuine products. Negotiating gives you a chance to find hidden treasures that might not be immediately apparent, as well as to purchase these treasures at a fair price. Astute bargainers may find one-of-a-kind gifts that contain unique significance and bring back treasured memories of their trip to Morocco because vendors frequently display their best items to them.

Contributing to the Local Economy: Bargaining actively contributes to Morocco's regional economy. Your purchases directly assist the vendors, artists, and their families. By haggling for a reasonable price, you can ensure that your purchase benefits the neighbourhood by giving artisans a living and preserving the local economy. It's a positive trade that goes beyond the souvenirs' just transactional worth.

Tipping is not expected

Morocco has quite different cultural customs and expectations from other nations about tipping. Although tipping may be expected or deeply engrained in many cultures worldwide, it is uncommon in Moroccan society. Instead, a variety of factors have influenced this unusual tipping strategy.

Tipping is not customarily anticipated in Morocco because many businesses build service fees into the cost of their products and services. By doing this, the original price of the service is paid, negating the need for extra tips from the clientele. Tipping is, therefore, not essential because the service charge is already included in the pricing on menus and bills.

Salaries and salaries: Moroccan service industry workers typically receive fair wages that are enough to support their livelihoods, in contrast to certain other nations where tipping is prevalent to supplement low wages. By doing this, employers may guarantee fair pay for the labour they perform and lessen the dependency on tips as a source of revenue.

Moroccans are known for their warmth and generosity in terms of hospitality. The idea of "douar," which means compassion or charity, is strongly established in society. Because of this, residents take great delight in offering top-notch service and hospitality without anticipating further financial compensation. This sincere hospitality goes beyond the requirement for monetary remuneration and is ingrained in the Moroccan way of life.

Avoiding inequities: The aim to prevent causing social injustices is another crucial factor. In Morocco, leaving a gratuity is occasionally viewed as a sign of affluence or social standing. There is a concerted attempt to advance equality and guarantee that everyone is treated with respect and dignity, regardless of their financial status, by not prioritizing tipping.

Cultural Protocol: It is vital to remember that Moroccan society still values good service even though tipping is not customary. It is permissible to express gratitude vocally or by saying "shukran" (thank you) if you are especially pleased with the service you received. This appreciation is frequently thought to be more significant than a tip.

Learn some Arabic phrases

Morocco is a fascinating nation renowned for its extensive history, vibrant culture, and breathtaking natural beauty. Learning a few Arabic phrases before you travel to this fascinating country will improve your trip and allow you to interact more meaningfully with the locals.

Morocco's official language, Arabic, is widely used daily, allowing you to immerse yourself in the nation's cultural diversity fully. You may engage in authentic conversations, show respect for regional traditions, and learn more about Moroccan culture by learning a few basic Arabic phrases.

First and foremost, Moroccan etiquette is based on Arabic greetings. The global salutation "As-salaam alaykum" (peace be upon you) will quickly close the communication gap between you and the locals. "Wa alaykum as-salam" (and upon you be peace) is the appropriate response to conclude the exchange of kindness. This small deed will demonstrate your goodwill and create a welcoming environment for future interactions.

It's important to express gratitude in interactions. Become familiar with the word "Shukran" and its variants, such as "Shukran jazeelan" (thank you very much) and "Shukran behalf" (a lot). By thanking people for their aid or acts of kindness, you'll foster a friendly atmosphere and leave a positive impression on the Moroccan people.

Learn language connected to necessities so you can move through daily encounters easily. "Min flak" (please) is a formal way to make a request, and "Ayna" (where) is useful for getting directions or finding certain locations. Pair it with the name of the place or landmark you're seeking, like "Ayna al-Medina?" (Where is the Medina?) You'll get some good advice from the people there.

Morocco is known for its distinctive flavours and aromatic spices; food plays a significant role in Moroccan culture. Knowing expressions like "La shukran, ana la azma" (No thanks, I'm not hungry) and "Tfaddal" (Help yourself/You're welcome to it) during dining will help you navigate mealtime customs and politely decline or accept offers of hospitality.

Lastly, haggling is a frequent activity when visiting vibrant markets or souks. Learn words like "Bshuf" (I'll look it over) or "Bi-kam hada"? The cost of this is to negotiate amicably and get the most out of your buying experience.

You'll be able to converse clearly and establish connections with locals if you spend time and effort learning Arabic phrases before visiting Morocco. By understanding the language, you will have a deeper grasp of Moroccan culture, gain insightful knowledge, and make lifelong memories. Take the plunge, learn the language, and use your Arabic phrases to help you discover Morocco's delights.

CHAPTER 5

Resources

Moroccan National Tourist Office website

For tourists looking to discover Morocco's numerous attractions, the website of the Moroccan National Tourist Office is a priceless resource. This extensive web resource is painstakingly created to offer a fascinating and immersive experience, reflecting the essence of this alluring nation in North Africa and motivating tourists to set out on a memorable journey.

The website's user-friendly interface, which makes navigating easy and entertaining, is one of the Moroccan National Tourist Office's most important qualities. Visitors are welcomed by spectacular images the instant they land on the homepage, showcasing Morocco's breathtaking landscapes, energetic towns, and cultural riches. The website features a sophisticated and contemporary design that captures the nation's distinctive fusion of heritage and modernity.

The Moroccan National Tourist Office website is a veritable informational gold mine, providing thorough information about the country's various regions, historical sites, natural wonders, and cultural events. Visitors can find complete itineraries, travel advice, and suggested activities to make the most of their trip to Morocco, whether they want to explore the historic medinas of Marrakech and Fez, unwind on the pristine beaches of Essaouira, or go hiking through the majestic Atlas Mountains.

The Moroccan National Tourist Office website stands out due to its dedication to authenticity and cultural immersion. The platform offers insights into Moroccan customs, gastronomy, arts, and crafts, going beyond simple tourist attractions. Visitors can discover the exquisite craft of Moroccan carpet weaving, learn how pottery is made using age-old methods, or even get a taste of Berber music's rich history. This focus on cultural awareness makes it possible for visitors to interact with the local populations and establish lasting relationships there.

The Moroccan National Tourist Office website also provides useful tools for tourists, such as details on visa requirements, travel choices, and a list of suggested lodgings, ranging from opulent resorts to comfortable riads. A hassle-free and well-planned journey is guaranteed by the website listing various tour operators and businesses that may help tourists arrange their itineraries or reserve guided excursions.

Through interactive features and interesting material, the Moroccan National Tourist Office website always seeks to improve the user experience. The website uses multimedia tools to transport visitors to the heart of Morocco and entice them to set off on their genuine adventure. These tools range from virtual tours of famous monuments to immersive videos that highlight the nation's vivid festivals and celebrations.

Printed in Great Britain
by Amazon

37255158R00056